Cranbury
Public
Library

23 North Main St. • Cranbury, N
(609) 655-0555

D1163515

I Like to Visit

The Zoo

Jacqueline Laks Gorman

Reading consultant: Susan Nations, M.Ed.,
author/literacy coach/consultant

WR WEEKLY READER
EARLY LEARNING LIBRARY

Please visit our web site at: www.earlyliteracy.cc
For a free color catalog describing Weekly Reader® **Early Learning Library's list**
of high-quality books, call 1-877-445-5824 (USA) or 1-800-387-3178 (Canada).
Weekly Reader® **Early Learning Library's fax: (414) 336-0164.**

Library of Congress Cataloging-in-Publication Data

Gorman, Jacqueline Laks, 1955–
   The zoo / Jacqueline Laks Gorman.
     p. cm. — (I like to visit)
   Includes bibliographical references and index.
   ISBN 0-8368-4456-4 (lib. bdg.)
   ISBN 0-8368-4463-7 (softcover)
   1. Zoos—Juvenile literature. I. Title. II. Series.
  QL76.G67   2004
  590.73—dc22   2004057438

This edition first published in 2005 by
Weekly Reader® **Early Learning Library**
330 West Olive Street, Suite 100
Milwaukee, WI 53212 USA

Copyright © 2005 by Weekly Reader® Early Learning Library

Art direction: Tammy West
Editor: JoAnn Early Macken
Cover design and page layout: Kami Koenig
Picture research: Diane Laska-Swanke

Picture credits: Cover, pp. 5, 7, 9, 13, 15, 17, 19, 21 Gregg Andersen; p. 11 © James P. Rowan

All rights reserved. No part of this book may be reproduced, stored in a retrieval system,
or transmitted in any form or by any means, electronic, mechanical, photocopying,
recording, or otherwise, without the prior written permission of the copyright holder.

Printed in the United States of America

1 2 3 4 5 6 7 8 9 09 08 07 06 05

Note to Educators and Parents

Reading is such an exciting adventure for young children! They are beginning to integrate their oral language skills with written language. To encourage children along the path to early literacy, books must be colorful, engaging, and interesting; they should invite the young reader to explore both the print and the pictures.

I Like to Visit is a new series designed to help children read about familiar and exciting places. Each book explores a different place that kids like to visit and describes what a visitor can see and do there.

Each book is specially designed to support the young reader in the reading process. The familiar topics are appealing to young children and invite them to read — and re-read — again and again. The full-color photographs and enhanced text further support the student during the reading process.

In addition to serving as wonderful picture books in schools, libraries, homes, and other places where children learn to love reading, these books are specifically intended to be read within an instructional guided reading group. This small group setting allows beginning readers to work with a fluent adult model as they make meaning from the text. After children develop fluency with the text and content, the book can be read independently. Children and adults alike will find these books supportive, engaging, and fun!

— Susan Nations, M.Ed., author, literacy coach,
and consultant in literacy development

I like to visit the zoo.
I like to watch the
monkeys at the
zoo. The monkeys
run and play.

I can see gorillas at the zoo. A gorilla is bigger than a monkey.

I can see lions, too. The lions are sleepy. They rest on the rocks.

I can see snakes at the zoo. A snake curls up on a branch.

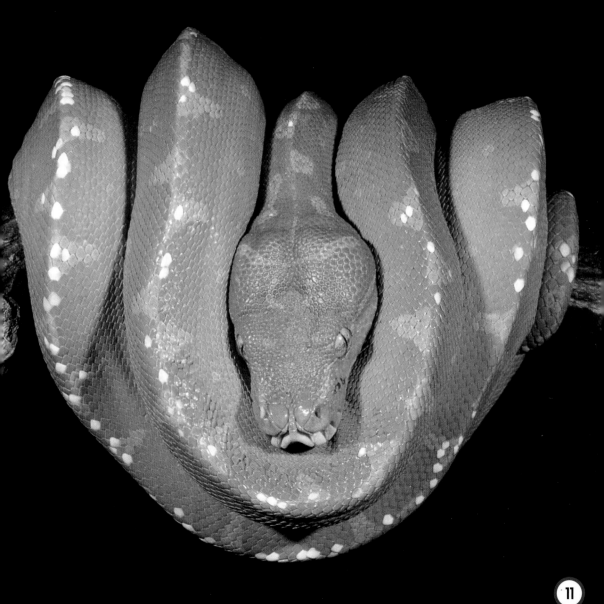

I can see bears at the zoo. Polar bears are the biggest, strongest bears. A polar bear swims in the water.

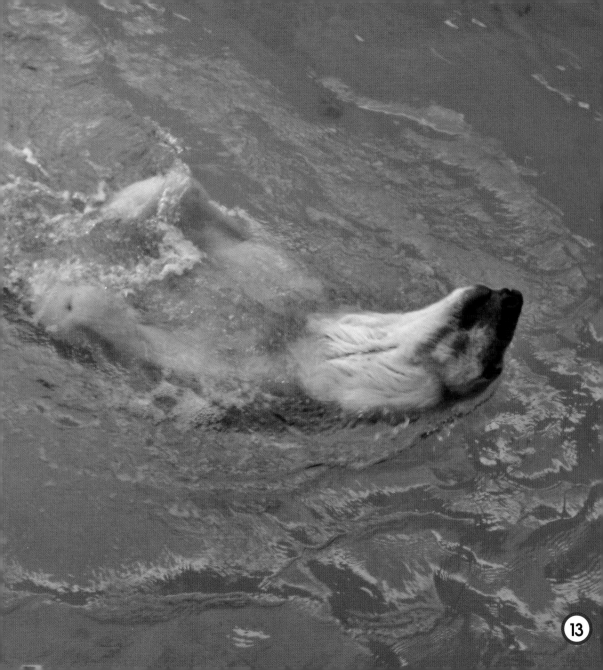

I like to see hippos at the zoo. Hippos are huge! A hippo wades in the water.

I like to see sea
lions, too. A
sea lion dives
into the water.

I like to go to the petting zoo. I like to pet the goats.

I like to see the giraffes, too. Which animals do you like to see?

Glossary

gorillas — large members of the ape family

hippos — (hippopotamuses) large African mammals with short legs and thick skin that live in or near water

monkeys — furry mammals that look like small apes, have hands and feet, and can climb and grasp objects

petting zoo — a place where children can pet and feed farm animals and other gentle animals

sea lions — large sea mammals that have thick fur and big flippers

For More Information

Books

Let's Go to the Zoo. Weekend Fun (series).
Cate Foley (Children's Press)

Monkeys. Animals I See at the Zoo (series).
JoAnn Early Macken (Weekly Reader Early
Learning Library)

Our Class Took a Trip to the Zoo. Shirley Neitzel
(Greenwillow Books)

A Trip to the Zoo. Karen Wallace (Dorling
Kindersley)

Web Sites

National Zoo
nationalzoo.si.edu/default.cfm
Pictures of the animals at the National Zoo in
Washington, D.C.

Index

About the Author

Jacqueline Laks Gorman is a writer and editor. She grew up in New York City and began her career working on encyclopedias and other reference books. Since then, she has worked on many different kinds of books and written several children's books. She lives with her husband, David, and children, Colin and Caitlin, in DeKalb, Illinois. They all like to visit many kinds of places.